Once Broken is captivating! Zanetta Collins is fearlessly transparent as she shares her journey to wholeness. This book reads like a movie script. Not only does it highlight the pain of overcoming your past, but at its core it highlights the loving commitment of our God who never gives up on his child. A must read!

Author Geremy Salter, Author of "Problem Causer, Problem Solver: The Next Move is Yours"

Once Broken

All rights reserved. No part of this book may be reproduced or transmitted in any form or by any means, electronic or mechanical, including photocopying, recording or by any information storage and retrieval system without permission in writing from the Publisher.
All scripture quotations are taken from
King James Bible, New Living Translation, NIV ®Copyright 2015 ©
[2009-2011]

Exert From the Poem " My Life As a Stud", by, Jackie Hill-Perry
Mention of Books: "When Heavens are Brass" By John Kilpatrick
"The Breakers Anointing" By Barbara J. Yoder
" Men Are from Mars, Women Are from Venus By John Gray

Self-Published (Collins Christian Co.)
Library of Congress Cataloging-in-Publication Data:
2016903960

Printed in the United States of America.
ISBN Number: **978-0-692-66059-1**
Memoir /Faith/Inspirational
Editing: Aretta Taylor Raines, Devonda Holloway
Pagination: Zanetta Collins
Cover Designed By: Micro Technologies /
http://microsol.biz/index.php
Bio Image: Zanetta Collins

Dedication

"Once Broken" is dedicated to the word perseverance as well as anyone who has fought the good fight. Just know that no matter how many times you may have fallen, you can still make a conscious decision. No matter what it looks like quitting is not, nor has it ever been an option!

It is also dedicated to those that have fallen and don't know how to get up. Get up and keep pushing! Faith is about moving forward even in your darkest hour. This book is a testament that no matter what the odds say, if you trust God, there is a healing in your soul waiting! I believe in you and more importantly, God believes in you!

Once Broken

Forward

As I read, Once Broken there were times I literally forgot that I knew Zanetta and I had a front row seat to her journey. This book vividly captures the essence of her intense desire to honor God while walking in and out of the struggles of her flesh and sin nature. The transformation from sin nature to Son nature was honest and compelling, making you remember why one would say YES to our Creator. It was refreshing, inspiring and transparent. I believe God was pleased as she poured out her pain it collided with her purpose.

This is a "must read" for anyone needing encouragement and a "go to" for those that doubt the power of deliverance.

Shauna K. Jackson

Once Broken

Acknowledgements

I would like to first thank my Apostle, Shauna J. Jackson as well as my Oil of Joy Church Ministries, Inc. family. It has been with great pleasure and honor to serve where I love. Apostle, your guidance has been parallel to none. I am truly blessed to have you as my cover, mentor and friend. Words could never express the depths of how I feel!

To my son, De'Vyon, thank you for being you! I am grateful for our personal journey together including all of the struggles and victories. They make us who we are. I am so excited about the man of God that you are! Even though you don't quite understand everything, keep moving forward in the things of God, and watch Him work in your life!

Most importantly, I would like to thank you Father God, for believing in me, even when I didn't have the strength to believe in myself. When most people figured I would fail, you saw something else. I might not like going through it in that moment, but you said, "*Zanetta, I am strengthening you, so hold fast my daughter! And even when you feel that you can't hold on, it ok fall on me, because I've got you!"*

About

Zanetta Lee Collins was born to Valerie and Luther Collins Jr. in Fort Ord, California. At the age of three, her parents divorced which forced her mother to relocate back to her hometown of Cocoa, Florida. Her mom later met and married (common law) Rudolph Murray who did his best to provide a stable home. Zanetta's childhood was turbulent and filled with strife. During her early childhood years, Zanetta suffered verbal and physical abuse and was molested by a family member when she was about 4 or 5 years old. Her mother was addicted to drugs nearly all of Zanetta's childhood into early adulthood.

This left a significant void in Zanetta's life. She felt disconnected, alone and always longed for her mother. Instead of allowing this pain to destroy her, she used this as a catalyst to improve her life. Determined not to follow in her mother's footsteps, she channeled her anger, hurt and frustration into excelling in athletics.

Zanetta excelled as an athlete and used sports as the gateway to a better education and a brighter future. Upon graduation from high school, Zanetta was awarded an athletic scholarship for basketball. However, during her journey, the residue of her past caused her to suffer from depression, anxiety and homosexuality.

While striving to obtain a college degree, she encountered additional obstacles and setbacks. She attended four different colleges while trying to find her way. During the process, she gave birth to a beautiful son, De'Vyon Collins. Due to sheer determination, after five years, she obtained her BA degree in Psychology from Edward Waters College in Jacksonville, Florida. Now with a degree in hand, it was still difficult to find stable employment to provide for her son. Shortly after graduation, she enlisted in the United States Army. This too would present a challenge as medical issues forced her to be medically discharged.

After being back in Cocoa for several years, the real journey began when she accepted the "Lord" as her personal Savior on August 18, 2009. This was undoubtedly the best decision she had ever made. It was not until this time she began the journey of discovering who she really was and who she really belonged to.

After giving her life to Christ, she attended cosmetology school and became a licensed cosmetologist. Afterwards, she then enrolled at Full Sail University to pursue her master's degree in Media Design, while establishing her new company ZLC, Incorporated.

Unfortunately, with only four classes remaining, she dropped out of school due to a clerical error at Veteran Affairs that stopped her from receiving financial aid funding.

She hasn't decided if she will return to finish her master's degree. Despite this, her life is evidence that no matter how severe the challenge, Zanetta will NEVER QUIT!

Once Broken

Introduction

God once said to me, *"You were created for such a time as this!"* When I heard those words I was in a resentful place in my life. But guess what? I quickly pick myself up off the floors and began to continue to move forward in the things of God. Now, did I always get it right? Absolutely not, but the one thing I did was never quit.

Since we last saw each other, I have been blessed too many times over to even count. Even though, I still haven't physically slept with another woman since we last spoke, I have still made mistakes. These mistakes shook me to the core.

However, these same mistakes have cause me to develop more wisdom, knowledge, and understanding of this thing called life. As well as living for a true and living God.

Welcome again into my persona journey, buckle up and get ready for round two of *"The Colors of My Wings"* entitled *"Once Broken."*

Once Broken

Once Broken

Table of Content

Dedication		23
Forward		25
Acknowledgement		27
About		29
Introduction		34
Chapter 1	The Breach	37
Chapter 2	The Takedown	54
Chapter 3	The Healing Chamber	88
Chapter 4	The Intro	107
Chapter 5	The Orders of My Steps	117
Chapter 6	His Way	135
Chapter 7	Don't Give Up Your Seat	146
Chapter 8	The Purge	163
Chapter 9	The No Quit Zone	171
Chapter 10	Closing Remarks	178

1

The Breach

So...now it's January 2013 and it's almost time for my autobiography to be released. Before the book's release, I'm taking a much needed vacation! My adventure will involve taking my first cruise. Ahh... I will have seven whole days of rest and relaxation in paradise. What can go wrong? I told myself that I deserve this trip. For the last 5 years, I have been serving God with all my heart. Surely I am strong enough to walk this thing out, so let's set sail! My bag is packed and I'm excited about seeing all these new places and I have no worries. We will be docking in the Dominican Republic, Puerto Rico and Bahamas just to name a few of the exciting stops. I am really enjoying myself from the great weather, chilled atmosphere and then...Boom! It hits me like a sucker punch out of nowhere, making me lose my mental and emotional balance. Like a thief sneaking up on an unsuspecting victim, that old familiar feeling, that tingling in my stomach caught me unaware. I feel a little lightheaded and my heart drops. I feel nauseous and nervous all at the same time. As I lifted my head, we made eye contact for all of two seconds, but it seemed like an eternity. Something says run but instead, I made eye contact and said, "Hi." She spoke back and immediately, I lower my head and quicken my pace to make sure no small talk occurred. Besides she was with a group of people which prevented a much needed escape. I was relieved because otherwise we might have ended up talking and it could have led to an extensive conversation. Then I said almost out loud, "ok *God, what is this?*" *"What's going on?"* *"Why do I feel this way God?" "Not again!"* *"I thought I was done with this! You SAID I was delivered! "*

My mind and heart was racing! I start talking to myself. *"Ok, Zanetta pull it together. This is a big boat. You don't have to be around her, ok? Relax and calm down. You've got this!"*

I made it through that day, but a few days later, my cabin mates and I headed out to take part in activities on the ship. *"Come on, Z, we are going to a spades tournament."* We get to the Spades tournament and I run right smack into the very person I thought I had escaped a few days earlier. She is across the room. And again we make eye contact and again my heart seems to take residence in my stomach. I felt as if the contents of my stomach were experiencing a civil uprising. *"God what's going on?"* "It was as if He wanted to reassure me. *"Now Zanetta, you can handle this. You are fine. You got this."* However, now I know that it was me just wanting to be ok, but I really wasn't. I was nowhere near prepared for what was coming.

We all commence to introduce ourselves to each other and have small talk during the tournament. *"Ok, see Zanetta, you've got this. You're cool. No worries. You're shooting the breeze with everyone!"*

She makes it a point to come over to me. *"Hello, my name is Kim,"* she greets me with a smile.

So I say, *"Hello, my name is Zanetta."*

Where are you guys from?"

We all answered her question and added the customary reply, *"And you? "*

"I'm from Georgia," she says.

We all continued to just have small talk. I learned later that she was one of the promoters for the trip. I was very impressed and I saw an opportunity to promote and gain exposure for my new book. This awesome book that God had given me for His people that would be used to break the chains of bondage and shatter the enemy's back. So...Boom! At least this is what I told myself.

She and I find a seat and start talking about my book and the release date. She responds, *"What is the name of your book? What is it about?"*

At this point, I know the enemy was trying me. However, I'm a fighter, so I'm going to prepare for battle. I knew enough to know the enemy was coming for me. Instead of using wisdom and avoiding confrontation by simply leaving, I go into strategy mode. Like a strategic card player, I pull out my big girl hand because I convince myself that running was a sign of weakness. Never mind that

I could clearly hear God telling me to go. In fact, he was telling me to RUN!

One who is wise is cautious and turns away from evil, but a fool is reckless and careless.

Proverbs 14:16

I find myself still sitting there flirting with temptation. I respond, *"Well the book is entitled, The Colors of My Wings. It is*
my autobiography."

She seems quite interested so I continue. *"It's a story of struggle, abuse, homosexuality and redemption."*

Once Broken

I then expressed my desire to help teach and empower kids so that they know they have the power to overcome any situation or circumstance.

Jesus said to him, if you can believe, all things are possible to him who believes.

Mark 9:23

I keep talking and stating my case like a witness on the stand. *"It's a story of pure love and real forgiveness."*

She was watching me intently. She responds with enthusiasm, *"Oh that's awesome! Well, we are going to announce that during the party we have tonight!*"

I am elated and I feel myself smiling. *"Oh, Wow! Ok, cool!"* I sat in disbelief at how easy that was to gain some more exposure for my book. *"I would greatly appreciate it."*

My friends come over and Kim and I continue to talk for a little while longer. Eventually, we all exchanged information and depart to go our separate ways. Later that evening we got dressed and prepared for the party. Now, by this time in my life I was not an avid partygoer. I thought to myself that I was on vacation and it couldn't do much harm to hang out and listen to some old school music. Anyhow, she had said that she would tell everyone at the party about my book. I went and it turned out to be a decent event. I danced a few minutes, but after about three songs, I sat down. Chilling and not really paying attention to who was around me, I look back on the dance floor. Can you guess who was in front of me dancing? At first, I acted as if I didn't see her, but she struts over to where I'm sitting. *"Hey lady, how are you are you? Are you enjoying yourself,"* she asked?

"It's cool," I respond. *"It's not really my environment, but I'm having a decent time."*

Kim quickly responds, *"Why are you not dancing?"*

I tell her, *"I did a little and that about it for me."*

She smiles, *"Ok, well I'm going back on the dance floor."* I smile back and say, *"Ok, enjoy!"*

She saunters back to the dance floor and starts back dancing. However, this time, instinctively, I knew she was strictly dancing for me. I sat there for a minute and when her back was turned, I just got up and retreated to my room.

I thought to myself as I took the long ride in the elevator to my room, *"Zanetta, what have you gotten yourself into?"*

I said to myself, *"I got to get off this boat, before I get in trouble."*

I was so naive because I still didn't realize that the enemy was trying to make a mockery out of me, my book, and everything I stood for. He wanted to laugh at my fight to live right, to be free, and he definitely didn't care about how far I had come in the last five years with everything in my life. After all, his whole purpose was to kill, steal and destroy. The saddest part was that God had forewarned me not to go on this trip.

So pay attention to how you hear. To those who listen to my teaching, more understanding will be given. But for those who are not listening, even what they think they understand will be taken away from them.

Luke 8:18

Once Broken

I didn't heed the warning because I saw no danger in taking a cruise. I told myself that I deserved a little vacation after all the things I had endured. Furthermore, I didn't want to see the danger in it (free will).

Don't be misled—you cannot mock the justice of God. You will always harvest what you plant.

Gal 6:7

We saw each other two more times. Once was on the beautiful beach in Turks & Cacaos, I purposely didn't speak. Then on the last day of my vacation, I caught a glimpse of her as we departed the cruise ship. As I exited the ramp to head back to reality, I said, *"Thank you, God! I dodged a bullet."*

2

The Takedown

After the cruise, I breathed a sigh of relief because I thought that I had avoided a major catastrophe. Ready, aim, fire...the enemy thought that I was target practice. On the other hand, that bullet that I thought that I dodged must have ricocheted.

I must have acquired selective amnesia, because I didn't remember that we exchanged numbers on the cruise. Even though we initially went our separate ways after the dancing fiasco on the ship, I think maybe a day went by and we were texting each other. I am not even sure who texted who texted first, but never the less we started communicating regularly.

At first, the communication was friendly small talk about nothing in particular. I thought to myself that she was cool and definitely funny. She was a very entertaining, smart and clever woman. She was into fashion, which I loved among other things. She also worked with battered women, which I thought was awesome. She had this fire and confidence that I have always been drawn to.

However, God said clearly to me, *"Zanetta ...RUN!"*

But once again I SAID, *"Zanetta, it's cool. Nothing is going on. You can handle it. What harm can it do? After all, you guys are nowhere near each other."*

The way of a fool is right in his own eyes: but he that hearkened unto counsel is wise.
Proverbs 12:15

And so it began....

Once Broken

But Samuel replied, "What is more pleasing to the LORD: your burnt offerings and sacrifices or your obedience to his voice? Listen! Obedience is better than sacrifice, and submission is better than offering the fat of rams.

1ˢᵗ Samuel 15:22

As the days went by, the chit chat or small talk evolved into extensive, long days and late nights of communication. With each day, our time spent talking increased like a small fire flamed by high winds. My desire for her began to grow while my strength to resist her advances was being destroyed by the destructive forest fire called lust. And just like a wild fire is hard to contain or put out, I couldn't stop the raging emotions in me.

I wanted to spend more and more time conversing with her. I would reassure myself that I had the right to talk to her by saying, *"man I am tired of being alone. There is nothing wrong with this because nothing has happened.* I am safe."

I guess you can compare it to when people are told to evacuate because some natural disaster such as a hurricane, flood or fire is headed in their proximity, but they ignore it. Honestly, I knew I was wrong, but my flesh was quickly taking over. About a month after meeting Kim, my head was spinning and my heart was torn between my love for Christ and my lust for this woman! It was a constant tug of war with me right smack dab in the middle.

A double minded man is unstable in all his ways.
James 1:8

And to top it all off, it was time for the release of my book, *"The Colors of My Wings."* I was feeling like a fraud, bigot, and a hypocrite. My mind was just going round and round in circles.

I wanted to just surrender to my desires, but I felt that I couldn't quit now because too many people were depending on me. They believed in me even though at that moment, I didn't believe in myself!

I did what I had to do and the book was released. I was blessed with so much support and it was such an amazing experience. It appeared that I was thriving with the success of the book. However, deep down inside I felt as if I was dying mentally, emotionally, and spiritually all over again.

During this time, I made up in my mind to end all communication with Kim. I told her we couldn't keep playing with fire. After all, fire burns. I told her that my life living as a lesbian was over. Also, I couldn't, nor did I even want to go back to living that lifestyle! Kim said that she understood but we still ended up talking that very day for about four hours!

I ended up again on this emotional roller coaster for refusing to heed God's warnings. To make matters worse, we started video chatting. I knew all I could hear was the Holy Spirit saying, *"Zanetta stop!"*

I know now what people mean when they say that they had a devil on one shoulder and an angel on the other. Even when I heard God beckoning back to the safety of his arms, *I* would hear the enemy say, *"There is nothing wrong with you being friends and talking to her. You're not doing anything wrong."*

Deep down, I knew in my heart of hearts that our relationship was wrong and nothing good could come of it. I did what anyone that likes to play with fire does...I continued talking and chatting with her. Everything about this was wrong, but like a fire being flamed by the wind, my desires grew and grew... a blazing inferno of lust and temptation.

Finally, my Pastor sat me down and said, *"Zanetta, what is going on with you?"* God was giving me the opportunity to expose the enemy, but I lied. I was crushed on the inside because I had never lied to Pastor until this day. Like the spiritual mother she is to me, she knew that I was not being honest and forthright. Apostle asked, *"Ok, Zanetta, when did we start lying to each other?"*

Unfortunately, all I could see was my failure, shame and setback. I had not only let her down, more importantly I let God down. I let the people down that believed in me and trusted the truth that dwelled in my loins.

She said, *"Zanetta, I see a wrench on your forehead twisting and turning your mind. So, talk to me."*

But I couldn't bring myself to tell her the truth. So, she said, *"Zanetta have you had sex with this woman?"*

I responded, *"No ma'am!" That was the truth,* but of course in my mind we had been intimate over and over again.

Set your mind on the things that are above, not on the things that are upon the earth.

Colossians3:2

My mind definitely was not thinking on the things that are above. Instead, it was fixated on this woman, Kim. More importantly, I had that sinful desire back in my head and like the richness of a sweet treats in my mouth, and I wanted her.

I couldn't look my Pastor in the face and tell her how I was feeling and the consuming thoughts that were raging within me!

She said, *"Well you're going to have to remove yourself from this woman, all form of contact needs to end now.*

I reluctantly agreed to her counseling, but honestly, I didn't stop. At that point, I wrote my Pastor/Apostle because I knew that I wasn't going to stop.

Dear Pastor,

I am writing you this letter because for some reason it seems to be very difficult for me to communicate my feelings. I do not know why that is. I know part of it is because you are my Pastor and the other part I think is because I do look at you as a mother figure and a friend, and I don't want to disappoint you or anyone but especially God.

As you well know it is my heart's desire to be obedient to 'God's will, His word and your authority. This is what makes this so difficult for me. I started doing things that are unacceptable and out of character for me which we have already discussed. I think I chose to write because I can never seem to get my feelings and thoughts out. Maybe it is also because I feel like a failure. There are so many things going on in my head and in my heart that some days I don't know whether I am going or coming.

I know that a big part of this is my fault because I entertained the attention that was given to me. Why? I am sure it is because of my loneliness that I have allowed this issue to literally bust me over my head. And yes, it has been really messing with my head and my thought process henceforth the vice grip!

You asked me a question the other day. Part of me didn't know how to answer and part of me was afraid to answer. You asked me what I wanted from the lady. Part of me wanted to tell you that I wanted to be with this woman, who is utterly absurd and crazy, I know. Because I know that that part of my life is over, I know that this is the enemy. I know in the natural that would never work and I know that in the spirit this situation is horrible. I know all of this, but yet I feel how I feel.

You said I have resentment and I do, some at me and some at God. I have been so frustrated with everything even though I see what God has been doing in my life and I feel wrong for that!

But I am doing my best to continue to be the open and transparent person that you have grown to love, but maybe I don't love myself, maybe I feel that's all I deserve. Do you have any idea what it feels like to hear all your life that you look like a man and you act like a man? And now to come to a place that you are called beautiful, but you look in the mirror and you still don't see what others see. All you see is what's not going on around you. You hear you have this new life ahead; but your body continuously reminds you of who you used to be. My desire is never to want a husband and still desire a woman. I always want to feel safe and secure in my surroundings and who God is creating me to be and be SECURE in that choice.

So what do I do? Go be a nun since being alone and away from the world seems to be the only way of safety for me? These are a few of the things that taunt me on a daily basis. I am so fearful of not overcoming and being who God has ordained me to be. Some days I feel like why not go back to what has always felt right to my flesh? Not to say I will, I am just saying this is what goes through my mind. As hard as I try, a lot of time I am uncomfortable in my own skin, which is sad. But all of these things are why I feel like I have resentment. I am just so frustrated and scared! It's very evident that I am not a big girl even though I so desperately desire to be. I pray that you and God both find it in your heart to forgive me for my previous indiscretions.

The one thing that is very much evident I have really come to understand that as strong as I think I am, I am not! I am weak! And I could never do this in my own strength. I could never, no matter how hard I try! But, anyway, I will do my best to continue to move forward in all things Christ-like!!!

Once Broken

> *Sincerely Motivated,*
> *Zanetta L. Collins"*

Even after the letter, the communication continued and the desire got deeper and deeper. It was destructive device waiting to be detonated.

We continued to communicate on the phone, texting, and now video chatting every night for hours at a time. I couldn't get close to her and now I am about to open myself up to more destruction. We then began having phone sex and from phone sex to "LIVE" video chat sessions basically making our own porn. The crazy thing is I had never been into or interested in porn. Nevertheless, I tried it a few times and I wasn't comfortable with it, so I stopped; but I never stopped her.

When you follow the desires of your sinful nature, the results are very clear: sexual immorality, impurity, and lustful pleasures.

Gal 5:19

Yet, God was still tugging on my heart and I could hear him saying, *"Zanetta, what are you doing?"* I couldn't look my pastor in the face. I couldn't look the people that trusted and believed in me in their faces…and let's not even talk about the book… What book? I felt that my book was a book of lies that I had created. However, remember this while you are reading this…"BUT GOD!"

He said to them, "I have noticed that your father's attitude toward me has changed. But the God of my father has been with me.

Gen 31:5

By this time I was over fighting my desires, fighting my flesh and trying to live right. I was going to get Kim and do whatever I needed to do to be happy. I had given up. Every time we made plans to meet in person, it never happened. There was always something that stood in the way of us connecting face to face from a broken down car to a lack of availability at the same time. During this process, I really began to understand the phrase; "God keeps you when you really have a desire in your heart to be kept."

"Don't be afraid," Moses answered them, "for God has come in this way to test you, and so that your fear of him will keep you from sinning!"

Exodus 20:20

I can be a witness to God hiding me under the shadow of His wing because it is true that he keeps you! She and I went around and around several more times about leaving each other alone, but it never worked. She understood my walk with Christ and didn't want me to walk away from God. I didn't want to walk away from God, but I began to feel so unworthy of His love. I was torn between two worlds.

Then one morning, for some reason, I ended up walking around in our local Target. I had no idea what I was there to purchase and just kept window shopping. While in the store, I got a call from my pastor. We began having an intense conversation. I can't even recall what it was about. I guess by the end of the conversation the floodgates had opened.

I was in tears and she questioned, "Zanetta, why are you crying?" I just told her that I didn't understand. I didn't understand why or how I was back in this situation. Basically, I was just tired of trying, tired of the fight. I wanted to give up and quit. I was over it. I was done!

We got off the phone and then my best friend Telma called. I was on my way from the store and we began talking. I broke down again. However, this time there was explosive anger and frustration.

"I can't do this, I'm tired, and I'm over this," I confessed to her.

"Zanetta, go to the beach and just talk to God," Telma urged me as she patiently let me vent.

"No! I might just walk out in the water and not come back," I screamed at her in the phone. That's just how hurt I was. In the end, I ended up at the one place that is my safe haven...the church.

At this particular time, my pastor had recently had surgery so I really didn't want to bother her. Although she was walking and moving around, she wasn't fully mobile yet.

I texted her and said, "Ok, I am at the church if you want to talk, I'll be here. "

Afterwards, I just turned my phone off. Before I knew it, I was on the altar crying my eyes out, yelling at God. I just kept asking why? I was literally on my knees, screaming at the top of lungs. I was really mad at God.

As I was crying out to God, in the fetal position and rocking like a baby, God said *"Why are you mad at me? I didn't do this. You did this not me."* He said, *"I told you not to do this."*

My sobbing began to slow. He said, *"You made your choice, now deal with it!"* My sobbing subsided even more and He said, *"You were created for such a time as this."* By now I was quiet. Then he said,

"Get up and do what I have called you do, because you were created for such a time as this."

So I got up, cleaned my face and sat there alone in the peacefulness of the sanctuary. My pastor never showed up at the church. I sat a little while longer waiting on her, so that I could come clean. I might have been there about an hour.

As I got ready to leave, I turned my phone back on. Several tiny little dings alerted me that I had several messages. Shortly after, my phone rang again. It was my spiritual mother, "Are *you ok,*

Zanetta? I tried to call you back. I can't drive right now, but God told me to tell you the conversation you two just had was between you and Him. He instructed me that all is well and stay home." I was ok by then and I knew that she had heard clearly from the Lord.

I still had to face Kim I texted her, but didn't feel the need to call. Yet I knew that she would call. If she called, I would talk though. Deep down, she knew just as well as I did that the lit fuse on that atomic bomb waiting to detonate had been drenched with the water of the Holy Spirit! This fiasco was at its end!

Ironically, I started having problems with my phone. For some reason, it wouldn't cut on. I didn't know what was causing the issue. That next Sunday morning we spoke briefly before I went to church. I remember it like it was yesterday because it was her birthday. I told her I was about to head to church. She asked about what time I was getting out. I sensed urgency in her voice. I told her the time and she told me that she would be busy during that time and I said, *"Well maybe I'll talk to you later."* She could feel me pulling away and she said, *"No, please just call me when you get out of church."* I reluctantly said agreed to call.

I headed to church and the anointing was on overflow. I ended up in my corner on my knees crying my eyes out, I mean just bawling! In the midst of it, I heard God's voice. He said, *"It's over."* And I said, *"Ok God, I'll tell her."* God said, *"No you won't. I said it's over and that means it's over NOW!"*

After church, I went home sat on sofa, grabbed my phone, and looked at her name and number for about ten minutes then I deleted her number. I knew, I knew, I knew that in that very moment as I hit that delete button, it was over! Afterwards, I picked up my phone and changed my phone number. I took another step of accountability by giving my Facebook and email password to a friend. I wanted her to intercept any communication and stand in the gap for me.

It was at that time that I began my healing process, but she still had my email address and she emailed and said, *"Well I hope your phone is just acting up because I haven't heard from you."* I looked at the email, but never responded.

Then a day later I got another email, *"Well Zanetta I emailed you on Facebook and your friend Ruby explained to me that we won't be communicating anymore because you feel that your relationship with Christ is the most important thing in your life. I love you and I will respect your wishes. Good bye.*

Once Broken

You see, I knew I couldn't truly live for Christ and go against His will for my life, I just couldn't do it. This was deeper than me and I had to hold on to that thought process for dear life if I was going to survive.

Accordingly, because you are lukewarm and neither hot nor cold, before long I will vomit you out of my mouth.

Rev 3:16

3

The Healing Chamber

My days continued and Kim was always on my mind and in my heart. Ultimately, I knew that nothing about that relationship with Kim would have been healthy or conducive for my *new life* or me. Without a shadow of a doubt, I knew that was not what God had in store for me. That part of my life was over and because I chose Christ! There was no looking back.

Once Broken

When they were safely out of the city, one of the angels ordered, "Run for your lives! And don't look back or stop anywhere in the valley! Escape to the mountains, or you will be swept away!"

Genesis 19:17

He believed in me even when I didn't believe in myself. There were other times when other people or even my family didn't believe in me; but I always knew that God was there waiting, anticipating and hold me close. At the very least, I desired to continue serving

Him with my obedience solely because He believed in me!

*"And now, Israel, what does the L*ORD *your God require of you, but to fear the L*ORD *your God, to walk in all His ways and to love Him, to serve the L*ORD *your God with all your heart and with all your soul, [13] and to keep the commandments of the L*ORD *and His statutes which I command you today for your good?*

Deut 10:12-13

Day-by-day it got a little easier. I began to understand "my truth" even the more.

I am crucified with Christ: nevertheless I live; yet not I, but Christ lives in me: and the life which I now live in the flesh I live by the faith of the Son of God, who loved me, and gave himself for me.

Gal 2:20

I began to understand that it's not about me. I am here to serve Christ to the fullest!

Those who belong to Christ Jesus have nailed the passions and desires of their sinful nature to his cross and crucified them there.

Gal 5:24

Then, an unexpected blessing dropped in my lap. There was a client of mine from my days of cosmetology school. She was an older lady that continued as my customer when I began working at the salon. One day, I was styling her hair and she said, *"Zanetta, have you ever thought of purchasing a house?"*

I quickly said, "No" and that I really had no desire to purchase a house at this time. In my mind, all I could hear was all of the issues such as maintenance that came along with purchasing a house. Also, I had no money to purchase or keep up a house. Most importantly, in my mind, the only reason I was still in Cocoa, FL was because of my ministry, *Oil of Joy*. I had received instructions from God to be still. My thought process was that the purchase of a home would lock me into never leaving Cocoa and I didn't want that. In retrospect, I see how simple minded we as people think. Our thinking is in a box, but my God is a God of greater than, not less than.

And God is able to make all grace (every favor and earthly blessing) come to you in abundance, so that you may always and under all circumstances and whatever the need be self-sufficient.

2 Corinthians 9:8

I really don't think I truly understood that about God until this woman that I barely knew said, "My husband and I recently came into some extra money. *We have already helped one family purchase a home and we would like to help you and your son purchase a home."*

I said, *"Ok, I will look."*

"Honestly, I didn't believe her or maybe I just didn't believe that she really wanted to do it for me. You know how people say a lot of things that never come to past. I just didn't want to be disappointed anymore in life. So, I glanced at homes here and there, but never really took the process seriously. Until one day while doing her hair again she said, *"So Zanetta, have you been looking for a house?"*

I said, *"A little"* and then I said, *"Ok, what exactly are you talking about Mrs. Miller?"*

She said, *"Well Zanetta, we helped another family get a home for $50,000* *and we want to help you and your son get one as well."*

"Mrs. Miller, you seriously want to help my son and me purchase a home for $50,000?" There was a joy springing up inside of me.

She said, *"Yes, go find you a house!"*

So I began seriously hunting for a home. I searched all over Brevard County. I had lived in Palm Bay, Florida before. I really enjoyed living there, so I started focusing in on that area. I found a home, but the home was $55,000. In my heart, I didn't want to ask her for more money after Mrs. Miller was already blessing me. Ironically, I heard God clearly say to me, just ask.

Ask and it will be given to you; seek and you will find; knock and the door will be opened to you.
Mat 7:7

I told Mrs. Miller that I had found a home, but it was $55,000.

Mrs. Miller said, *"Ok, let me talk with my husband Randy and see what we can do."*

A few days later, she called me back. I was a little apprehensive and not sure that she would agree to the price since it was over the amount that she had given me.

"Ok, Zanetta, we will do the $55,000."

By this time, my mouth literally just dropped and I know that my eyes had to be like flying saucers. In my head, I'm questioning God. *What are you doing? Better yet Lord, why are you doing this for me?*

I began to realize that because of my faithfulness and obedience to Christ and His will for my life, he chose to reward me for my faithfulness. It may be difficult for some to fathom the depth and degree of my blessing. You see, I had a credit score of 530, two repossessions and countless collections on my credit. There was no way that I, Zanetta Collins, could walk into a bank and get a lender that would have approved me for a home.

Know therefore that the LORD your God is God, the faithful God who keeps covenant and steadfast love with those who love him and keep his commandments, to a thousand generations.

Deuteronomy 7:9

So I attempted to get in contact with the seller and after a week of back and forth negotiations, the seller decided to take the house off the market and use it as a VA starter home for disabled veterans. Ironically I laughed to myself, because I am a disabled veteran! However, I had no idea who to contact and neither did the seller. I didn't totally understand how the seller had no idea who to contact when it was their house. Nevertheless, it was back to the drawing board. I started looking again for my house. In the meantime, my lease at my apartment was just about up.

One evening I was in church waiting on the service to start, my phone rings. It was funny because I never answer my phone when I am in service, but I did this particular time.

In my mind, I thought that since we hadn't quite started, I answered. It was one of the realtors I had searching for a home for me. She said, *"Hey Zanetta, there is home that hasn't even hit the market yet. I am about to put it up on the*

"MLS" today. I think you should go and check it out."

After church, I hurried over to the location of the home. I didn't really care for the neighborhood. However, I got lucky or blessed depending on your belief system. I say blessed. When I got to the house, the owners were working inside. They allowed me to walk through the home. Even though I didn't like the neighborhood, I liked the house. I asked if they would take cash. They said, "Sure."

Afterwards, I contacted Mrs. Miller and we began the process to buy my first home. Thanks to God and His earthly angel, Mrs. Miller and her husband Randy, I was going to own my first home. My son and I purchased our first home for $47,500 with a credit score that was well under 600. The interest rate on my home was under 6% and my mortgage payments were set for a 20-year period with a monthly payment well under a 1-bedroom apartment. Mrs. Miller also gave me the remaining balance of about $5,500 after paying everyone that had to be paid during the transaction. After receiving the extra money, I began repairing my credit and I also purchased my homeowner's insurance.

Afterwards, my old trusted 1994 Ford Taurus broke down and I had to find a car. I didn't want any car payments. So I searched and searched for a car, but I couldn't find anything that I knew would truly be dependable. I happened to be on the phone with one of my sisters in Christ and she said, *"Zanetta, I am taking you to the bank to try and get a loan for a car."*

I said, "Man, these people are not going to give me any money with my credit."

She said, "Zanetta, it is a new season!"

Reluctantly, I went to the bank still not really believing that I would be approved for a car loan. While waiting to be seen by the loan officer, I just began praying *"Ok God, I really don't want a car payment especially with this new home. Of course, if it's your will, I'll take it. All I ask God is please keep my payments at $200."* Then my name was called.

"Hello Ms. Collins, let us see if we can get you in a car today." We sat down and went through all of your financials. I ended up with a new car with only three years of payments with single digit interest rate. And yes, my car payment was pretty *close* to what I asked God for! I mean you couldn't get closer, if you threw a dart at it. I smiled and thought that it was not bad for a girl with a credit score under 600, right? Nope, because my God can do anything if you just believe!

Once Broken

I can do all things through Christ who strengthens me.

Phil 4:13

My reason for telling you this is so you never forget that you have to believe in our God. He is far greater than we can imagine. God began wooing me, showing me the power of obedience. *"If you are obedient to me, I will bless you far greater than you could ever imagine."* I never looked back again after that day.

4

The Intro

After the purchase of my new home I had a few issues with the plumbing. I had a childhood friend that was a plumber. I called him up to come and check out the plumbing in the house. I had always thought that he was cute. When I was younger, I typically preferred a tall guy, but he was about 5 feet 8, inches tall with brown eyes. He seemed to be a very humble guy but he was much younger than me. Even before he came to work on my house, I would run into him around town. Several times, he even did work on my mom's house. I saw him so much that I thought maybe God was giving me a sign and nudging me to say something. Every time he saw me, he would just shake my hand and stare. You know that hand holding that happens when you don't want to let go or that stare that someone like me would shy away from; this would happen every single time we saw each other. I even asked my pastor what she thought about a woman asking a man out on a date. I wanted to make sure because I use to date women and I knew that I still had a little of that aggression in me that might not be attractive to a man.

He who finds a wife finds what is good and receives favor from the LORD.
Proverbs 18:22

Shoot, I was shocked that I was actually at the point of being intrigued and attracted to a man! I know that may sound crazy. My Apostle and I talked about it and she just stated that *"She wouldn't recommend it to all women, but hey Zanetta go for it!"*

Well he was at my house working in my bathroom in my room and I kept him company and talked for a while. I thought about asking him then; but I was like, "No we are in my bedroom and I haven't had sex in five years, so this might not be wise. I decided to wait. We continued talking until he finished. As we walked out of the room I said, *"Ok, Zanetta, it's now or never."* As he was about to leave, I stopped him and asked him if he would like to go out on a date sometime? I was so nervous. Especially after the situation with Kim because it made me feel as if I wasn't ready to date.

He said, "Yes!" But, then I didn't hear from him for a while. It took about two months for us to go on that date. Eventually, we went on a date and it was great! He was a respectful gentleman. I said, *"Wow, I can do this!"* I actually had butterflies in my stomach. Inside, I was a nervous wreck. I wanted to burst out in tears, but not tears of sadness. They were tears of joy because I was able to see the manifestation of what God was doing in my mind and my soul. I was excited about the excitement even in my body. It was literally blowing my mind!

He and I began spending more and more time with each other. Yet every now and then, he would play the *"disappearing act"* and to me that was a red flag. I wanted to run, but my Pastor said, *"Zanetta don't run."*

I told her I was tired of being hurt and really didn't want to ever be hurt again, but she said, *"If he hurts you what's going to happen? You will heal!"*

I said, "Ok" so I didn't run. I stayed and slowly but surely my walls began coming down. When we spent time together, he treated me like a queen when I was in his presence. On the other hand, *Mr. Disappearing Act* did what he does best every so often...disappear.

By this time, I had had enough. I was over it and I was done. After eight months of not running away and doing things his way, I basically told him that whatever we had going on between us was over! You see, in Christ you begin to understand your worth. You start understanding the true meaning of that phrase "Who I am and who's I am."

But I didn't do it, for I acted to protect the honor of my name. I would not allow shame to be brought on my name among the surrounding nations who saw me reveal myself by bringing the Israelites out of Egypt.

Ezekiel 20:9

You see I am glad I didn't run because spending time with him helped draw out the femininity that had been lying dormant all those years. It showed me that I could allow a man to love me.

It also showed me that I didn't have to settle for less than my worth.

He was a good guy just not the good guy for me. I also understood that I didn't have to settle which used to be an issue for me when I dated women. I would try to be everything other person needed, yet it was never enough. I would hang around like a puppy dog expecting the next person to realize my worth. The problem with that was I had to realize my value. I had to realize that in Christ I am worthy. I am also glad that I didn't run from him because it also taught me that I could withstand hurt and pain and still walk away whole and intact as a woman. If I had not been in Christ dealing with him, the experience would have left me broken…again.

5

The Ordering of My Steps

By this time, work had gotten slow and book sales had slowed down as well. I began feeling a tug on my heart to leave the salon I was at and move to a barbershop, but I had no clue where to go. I knew people that owned barbershops, but was it the right barbershop for me? So, I stopped working at the salon and for the most part, I just stayed home.

I felt like I was falling into a depression. At the same time I knew what God had for me, so I did my best to wait patiently. Then another blessing was presented to me by my friend Jasmine, *"Zanetta, some friends of mine own their own barbershop in Titusville. They are looking for a new barber and they are men of God."*

I said, *"I don't know Jasmine."* *My mind was all over the place, I was scared. Why? I don't know!*

She said, *"You have to meet with them."*

So I drove to Titusville and while sitting in my car, my phone rings. It was Jasmine. She talked to me for a few minutes telling me to be calm and go in with confidence. Then someone else got on the phone and she said, "I have a word for you." She said, *"God told me to tell you that this new place, this new job is for you. It's going to catapult you to where you want to be."*

After getting off the phone with her, I called my Pastor. I sat in my car and prayed with my Pastor then we got off the phone. At that point, I just began to cry. I knew this was what would be needed to move me forward to this new place in business. God had given me big dreams and this was the second step toward reaching some of my goals business wise!

"For I know the plans I have for you," declares the LORD, "plans to prosper you and not to harm you, plans to give you hope and a future."

Jeremiah 29:11

I began working at *Kingdom Cutz* in Titusville, Florida alongside two of

Brevard County's top barbers under the tutelage of Pastor Daryl and Minister Delvin Smith. Day- by- day, I took my time and began honing my skills. The funny thing is that after I began working there, I realized there were a number of reasons God orchestrated this job for me. God also placed me at *Kingdom Cutz* because it gave me a chance to learn more about the "Male species." So, instead of me trying to be this man that I would never be, now I could learn how men act, how men think, what makes them upset, what makes them smile etc...

This is all in preparation for when my Boaz walks into my life. Communication between the two of us won't be so hard because I am privileged to learn in the midst of all these men. It is true, although I have never read that book, *"Men Are from Mars, Women Are from Venus."* I understand it now because we communicate differently. Sometimes that lack of being able to express how you truly feel to the person you love most can destroy relationships. I have already started praying about the communication between me and my future husband. That has been a prayer of mine because the word tells up to write it down and make it plain.

And the LORD answered me:

"Write the vision; make it plain on tablets, so he may run who reads it.

Habakkuk 2:2

Another one of the prayers that I have written down concerning my Boaz is that we have an unusual level of communication. This means that we will be able to sit and talk things through and have a precise understanding of how each other may feel about any given subject! I am grateful that being at *Kingdom Cutz* has given me the opportunity to learn from these Godly young men.

Sometimes when it was slow at work, my co-workers, Delvin (a Minister), his brother Daryl (a Pastor) and Geremy (also a Pastor) and I would literally have sessions about so many things including work, growth, ministry, God and relationships. They would talk to me about where I was in my own headspace, at times. It is truly a blessing for me to be able learn about myself, grow and continue to become the woman that God is shaping and molding me to be.

"I praise you, for I am fearfully and wonderfully made. Wonderful are your works; my soul knows it very well. My frame was not hidden from you, when I was being made in secret, intricately woven in the depths of the earth."

Psalms 139:14-15

I also believe my relationship with these men has taught me that there are truly some Godly men out there that are faithful. Not only are they servants of Christ, but servants in their homes. I don't say much unless I am asked; but I sit back and I watch how these men cater to their wives and work so hard to provide them with not just a stable home but also, a future! This is awesome to me.

I also learned lessons in the strength of vulnerability. You see I hated being vulnerable. I have always had to be the *strong* one. Dealing with a mother suffering from addiction, I had to be the one to be strong and look out for my sister. I could never let her see me cry.

She had to know that no matter what we were going through that we would be ok because I had her back! I had to be the strong one in my previous relationships with women. Why? Because they were all broken and I had to be the mender. Why? (By the way, that never happened.) Not only was I also broken, but time and time again, relationship after relationship, we both were left in a more broken state than we had been originally. That basically means that we ended up being worst off than we were before we had a relationship.

Once Broken

There is a young poet by the name of Jackie Hill-Perry. Her poetry was introduced to me about six months after I gave my life back to Christ by one of the Ministers in my church, Minister Devonda Holloway. She is an awesome Psalmist and a fabulous God Chaser. She calls me and says, "Sis, you have to watch this video!" The name of the video is "*My Life as a Stud,*" and I think that she (Jackie Hill) at the time said it best. In the poems she says:

"You know what's dangerous about being a stud? We not only affect ourselves but also affect all the

chicks that we lay with. We spend our whole relationship with that "fem" or "stem" or whichever you choose, by trying to make up for all the people that left her heart bruised. We become that father that left too soon. We become that dude that hit and quit after school. We become that mother that had too many rules, by becoming the God that she is suppose to worship on Sunday afternoon. We take on the task of pasting together every piece of her that has been broken and when we leave those pieces that we held on so tightly in our hands fall to the floor patiently waiting, on the next person to come through the door, leaving her more broken than she was before."

When I tell you that is one of the most profound insights that I have ever heard concerning my previous choice to live as a homosexual. This entire poem had me in tears! You really should look her up on the internet because this little excerpt doesn't do it justice. Ok now back to my story.

Not only on a personal level, the positive impact of being employed at Kingdom Cutz has spiraled to other areas besides my personal life. Though Daryl and Delvin's insight, it has definitely helped drive me to higher heights be it

Ministry, business as well as relationships! When I came into their shop, I quickly realized that these men were motivated business men that not only wanted better for themselves, but better for the community. I knew beyond a shadow of a doubt that God had placed me in the right place! I have this motto that I have heard several times, *"Keep yourself around like minded people."* These guys are like-minded people, Men of God, motivated to excel in all things. That is who and what I want to be around me at all times. The word tells us that we are our brothers' keeper. I feel as though these guys have supported me, looked out for me and taught me so much.

" For I was hungry and you gave me something to eat, I was thirsty and you gave me something to drink, I was a stranger and you invited me in, needed clothes and you clothed me, I was sick and you looked after me, I was in prison and you came to visit me.

Matthew 25:35-36

The King will reply, 'truly I tell you, whatever you did for one of the least of these brothers and sisters of mine, you did for me."

Once Broken

Matthew 25: 40

Why? Because these guys saw things in me that I didn't quite know how to pull out of myself. For instance, after one particular conversation about some ideas that God had placed in me, Delvin said, *"Zanetta, you need to look up a friend of mine. She has an awesome testimony. Her name is Tekoa Pouerie. I think that developing a relationship with her could be a blessing for you."* I agreed and looked her up on Facebook and sent a friend request. Every so often I would look her up and read about her.

This woman is a married mother of two, a minister, a motivational speaker, an author who has written six books, not to mention the owner of a million dollar company. I wanted to reach out to her, but at the time, I really couldn't afford to pay her for her services. I hesitated and shied away from contacting her. Then one day, I just stepped out on faith. I trusted that if this is what God has for me He would make a way for me to afford her coaching services.

6

His Way

In the midst of me stepping out on faith my Pastor, (now Apostle) had preached a sermon entitled *"Wake Up."* The sermon basically addressed that God's people had been asleep and it was time to wake up. She stated that businesses were being birthed in this season. This was all the more confirmation for me because God had been dealing with me about my business and even about me conducting public speaking engagements. I began speaking again at events, sharing my testimony. During those engagements, it gave me further opportunities to share my book *"The Colors of My Wings"* while sharing the goodness of God. I was so excited about what God was doing but I was also very confused. I was confused because initially I thought God was birthing me in ministry within my home church and it hurt to find out that that wasn't his plan for me. And the funny thing is I never wanted to have a title or become a Minister. Still and yet, I was hurt and even began to grow bitter which was a snare:

Therefore I will not refrain my mouth; I will speak in the anguish of my spirit; I will complain in the bitterness of my soul.

Job 7:11

It's a good thing that I recognized it. I just sat down and spoke with my Apostle about it. She just confirmed again what I kind of knew already: that God was using me for something different and I needed to build what God was birthing in me which wouldn't take away from my service to God or my church home. I understood the words that came from her mouth, but I still hadn't had that light bulb moment. Therefore, I continued on and began moving in the direction that God was leading. It was at that time that I reached out to meet with Mrs. Pouerie.

When I reached out to schedule the appointment, I was so anxious. I had to wait two or three weeks for our first appointment. We scheduled the first appointment but then we had to reschedule because she had an emergency. We tried several more times to reschedule because of an unexpected funeral that she had to attend. By this time I was aggravated and frustrated...BUT GOD! Finally, we were able to have our first meeting. She and I met and I was in heaven! I was so excited to again be around someone that was like minded, driven, and focused; not just on the things of God but also the gifts that God had placed in her. I was motivated to say the least! She apologized for the delays, but I know that everything happens in God's timing!

Once Broken

For still the vision a waits its appointed time; it hastens to the end—it will not lie. If it seems slow, wait for it; it will surely come; it will not delay.

Habakkuk 2:3

After our first meeting, I met with my team of people that I usually consult with. I told them about the meeting we had and that we needed to prepare for the next meeting. I just knew that I was supposed to work with this lady.

After the next meeting, my best friend Telma said, *"Did you hear what Tekoa said?"* She said, *"It's time to wake up!"* I didn't even catch it, but that was the defining moment for me. This was a divine appointment because again my Apostle had recently preached on waking up!

To everything there is a season, and a time to every purpose under heaven.
                              Ecclesiastes 3:1

So we began working together, she would instruct and I would move. She would instruct and I would move, but the more I worked, the more the process seemed to consume me. I was beginning to get drained and I didn't know why. And then a word came..."Zanetta, you have an unnatural weight on you."

I said, "Well what does that mean?" Here it was that I am being as obedient as I know how, trying not to do things in my own strength. I KNEW me meeting this woman was ordained by God; yet my body had begun to shut down. However, I didn't want to stop.

I didn't want to quit. As I sat pondering how to call this woman who has been such a blessing in my life and in this season, I get an email. *"Hello Zanetta, due to extenuating circumstances we are going to have to put a hold on coaching for now."*

You see I was struggling with letting go…struggling with backing up, struggling with slowing down…In my mind there was no way I had come this far to see the finish line but not be able to cross it. However, God said not yet…and He knew that because of who I was that that would be a hard thing because He created me, so he did it for me.

You made all the delicate, inner parts of my body and knit me together in my mother's womb.
Psalm 139:13

Once Broken

Instantaneously, I began sleeping better and having more energy. It is crazy how God does things He knew that I wasn't ready, even though my heart was right. I just wasn't ready for what He had for me!

Don't worry about anything; instead, pray about everything. Tell God what you need, and thank him for all he has done.

Philippians 4:6

I hated where I was despite what I had accomplished. I still despised where I was. I JUST DIDN'T GET IT! I kept hearing "Be ready, be ready, be ready. Be prepared to move when God says move." In my eyes that was all that I had been doing.

However, then God told me, *"You are not seeking me in the process you are trying to do this in your own strength and it can't be done in your own strength."* Of course, I was a little resentful. The more I thought about it the more resentment built up in my heart and in my mind!

7

Don't Give Up Your Seat

Despite my feelings and regrets, I continued to obey God's word. By this time, spiritually in this season, we as a ministry (and as individuals) were being confronted with that one thing…that one thing that kept you bound in your past; that One Thing that will either cause you be who you say you are or break! As believer we could either stand on the true and living word as your foundation or fall and that one thing for me was the spirit of homosexuality!

"I know all the things you do, that you are neither hot nor cold. I wish that you were one or the other! But since you are like lukewarm water, neither hot nor cold, I will spit you out of my mouth!"

Revelation 3:15-16

With that being said, like always, a snare had been set; and it was time for me to either put up or shut up pertaining to who and what God has called me to be! My first snare was not realizing what season I was in. I met a young lady who seemed fun and we had great conversation, I basically looked at her as someone that I thought I could be cool with.

God quickly said, *"NO" Remove yourself!"* My ears were closed and I didn't catch it! I thought it was me just over exaggerating. In my head, I had clearly been doing this long enough to never have desires for another woman ever again in life. The funny thing is I don't but this is why we as Christian have to pay attention and not just Christians! We have to be able to identify the real issue at hand. At that moment, it had nothing to do with the spirit of homosexuality; it had to do with the spirit of loneliness!

Be determined and confident. Do not be afraid of them. Your God, the Lord himself, will be with you. He will not fail you or abandon you."

Deuteronomy 31:6

You see for someone who was a "serial monogamist" being alone had never been my thing before Christ. I'd venture to say that it hadn't been my thing after Christ either! What I will say is that over the last seven years I have learned to handle that loneliness a little better; but it does hit me every so often!

Ok, so now back to my new acquaintance... She was cool, but again God said "No." You do not need to be around her and like I said before, I didn't realize that's what God was saying to me. She and I began spending time around each other. Initially, I didn't know any of her past story. The one thing I could see very clearly was that she wanted me. If I wanted her, I knew I could have her. Ironically, I had no desire or taste for this woman! This means that if you knew me before Christ, you would know. Even if you read my first book, "The Colors of my Wings" you would know that I had an insatiable appetite for women! You would also know that when I came to Christ, throughout my struggles and my deliverance process, my mouth would water for the intimacy of a woman,

But each person is tempted when he is lured and enticed by his own desire.

James 1:14

... I guess that I no longer had those desires; I no longer had that taste. However, the spirit of loneliness was lurking and because I had gotten distracted.

Keep your eyes straight ahead; ignore all sideshow distractions.

Proverbs 4:25

The levee had been weakened and the breach had been created! Very quickly our relationship became strained! Every conversation had become egregious and overwhelming. But I wanted to be that light...that light in a dark place because she needed Christ just like all of us.

Once Broken

But God said, *"Zanetta she isn't your assignment in this season."* This time when He said it, I caught it. I quickly removed myself! Even though nothing happened, I had been weakened and distracted on the task at hand and the major test before me!

And so it begins… frustrated and distracted, my mind was clearly not focused on God. Despite all that I had accomplished to this point and praising God about how far I had come and all the miraculous blessings that He had performed in my life, I was in a scary place. I was focused on where I wasn't or what I hadn't accomplished or even the fact that I remotely thought of sleeping with a woman ever again in life. This lack of being focused and that distraction had taken me off course; a course that could have derailed and discredited who I have become. Of course, the ultimate temptation was a new woman!

You see, the enemy never comes with something new to tempt you it's always something old. We have to be able to identify it when it approaches.

"Behold, I give you the authority to trample on serpents and scorpions, and over all the power of the enemy, and nothing shall by any means hurt you."

Once Broken

Luke 10:19

Keep in mind the levee has already been weakened and the breach had been opened!　There was this woman I had known for quite some time. We had known each other for years, we had a brief interaction years and years ago; but now she was seemingly saved and happily married with six kids. She had a husband who was a great provider and she just seemed to be happy. As far as I knew, I was the only woman that she had been with. Now she was back in my life! Why? I asked, but I got no answer for the time being. We started out just chatting and being cool like all my previous relationships. She even asked if she could purchase one of my books, "*The Colors* of My Wings." I just figured she wanted to see if she was in the book, (even though she wasn't)! After she read the book, it seemed to open her up to our past and our old life, which wasn't my intention!

When I wrote "The *Colors of My Wings*" it was a purging of sort. Despite the many compliments that I received about the book, from it being a great read, very insightful or helpful, I never thought about the flip side of it. It could open up a can of worms for people who dealt with sexual sin and basically rehash old mindsets. It really never crossed my mind and for that I apologized because that wasn't my intentions!

Yet again the breach had been first opened by me with the previous situations. As before, we began hanging out we had a few girls' days out. Nothing major. One day as we were having a conversation. I can't even say that it was a serious conversation. As I sat up in my seat, she looked at me and sat back. In that very moment, I knew that we had a serious problem.

Once Broken

Catch the foxes for us, the little foxes that spoil the vineyards, for our vineyards are in blossom."

Solomon 2:15

In that brief moment, we tried to over look it, but that wasn't going to happen for long. In our conversations, I realized how unhappy she seemed in her marriage, but I really couldn't understand. Here it was she had a loving husband who was a great provider, but yet you're unhappy? I didn't get it! Something else I have learned in my life that I can't save everybody. When I was in the world, I wanted to be that protector, that person that always had your back. I was that person in all my relationships no matter what kind of relationship it was!

So, I'm sitting here thinking, "Ok, what's going on why am I here again? "

I just don't understand it. I had no desire what so ever for this woman. Yet I knew that all I would have had to do is say," Yes and it would have been on and popping! As I explained earlier though, it was the loneliness that tried to draw me. Part of me wanted to run, but then there was another part of me that refused to run! I didn't know what to do so I started actively praying for her and her marriage. Every day, I would pray for her, her marriage and children. I can't lie it was hard because that loneliness seemed to be taking over. I kept hearing don't run, but everything in me wanted to scream and take off running. There was something in me that kept saying, *"If you run you will be running for the rest of your life.*

In that moment, I stood still. I told her straight up, *"Ok let's just say that we did sleep together? It's not going to change a thing. It is only going to get worse on both of our ends."*

I would have ruined yet another marriage. She would have committed adultery. All of the problems in her marriage would have still been there. Once we would have gotten out of that bed, I would still have to answer to God for my choices of allowing my flesh to rule me. I just couldn't have that on my conscience! Therefore, I continued to pray for her and her marriage. It seemed as if the enemy was saying, *"It is ok, no one will ever know, do it just one time!"*

Then I would hear God say, "No: Stand! You've got this!" By no means am I a Job, but this scripture came to mind.

Then the Lord said to Satan, "Have you considered my servant Job? There is no one on earth like him: he is blameless and upright, a man who fears God and shuns evil."

Job 1:8

That's the scripture that continued to come to mind. Now, that's not to say that I did everything right, who does? But, I fought, and fought and I refused to quit no matter how hard it was. I was determined to be that light in a dark place. I am a servant and believer in Christ! The least that I can do is be that light!

"Let your light shine before men in such a way that they may see your good works, and glorify your father who is in heaven." Matthew 5:16

8

The Purge

During this process, I was attending 6:00 a.m. prayer. One morning a woman that I had never met happened to be attending prayer. I looked at her and she looked at me. She seemed a little different, so as she watched me I watched her. When prayer ended, she walked up to me and we introduced ourselves. Then she reached in her backpack and handed me a book entitled, *"When Heavens Are Brass"* by John

Kilpatrick. She said, "God told me to give you this, but I don't know what's in it."

I said, "Ok thank you!" I took that book and I read it cover to cover! The book talks about obedience, choices, why our prayers don't seem to reach heaven because of our disobedience. This is why "The Heavens Are Brass, and Revival!"

This book was very insightful and influential in me continuing to be rooted and grounded in my faith! A few days later, I was on my knees praying but I was struggling to connect with God. She walked over to me and said, "Zanetta, come and sit right here. There is a blessing right here." Because I really didn't know her I looked at her like she was crazy. I still got up and sat where she told me to sit, even though I did it with pause. She sat down next me and we began talking about marriage and healing.

She explained to me that when God heals a person's heart it's not super glued together. Instead it is completely mended, no visible crack, no scars and you are healed completely! Once she finished talking, she got up and continued to pray.

Once Broken

I stretched out on the floor and began to pray. I prayed like never before! I prayed for almost an hour, crying and sweating! Something was going on in my body. My heart began pounding and pounding. Then finally it was quiet.

After prayer I came home and again something else began to take place. Unbeknownst to me, I had no clue that a purge had begun during prayer and continued for two days. My mind was blown with what God was doing in me. It is kind of hard to explain, so I'll say it like this. That day my heart was healed and any desire that I may have had for a woman was completely removed in those two days! Not sure how many of you have ever read the book "*The Breakers Anointing*," by Barbara Yoder; But that is the best way to explain it. I truly believe that the "Break" swept through my mind, my body, and my heart and completely removed any residue of the old me as if it never existed!

Afterwards, I called up my friend and told her about my experience. It was if whatever was downloaded in me began to download in her. From that day on, the temptation to sleep together had completely disappeared. All I could say was thank you Jesus!

The Bible says: *So humble yourselves before God. Resist the devil, and he will flee from you.*
James 4:7

And that's exactly what I did! Was it hard? Yes! Was it painful? Yes! Was I weak? Yes, extremely! There were times when I didn't know if I was going to make it! If I was going to be able to stand firm, I was so weak! But, that's what God wants from us. He wants us to seek Him

Once Broken

in our weakness, so His glory can be revealed in us! In our weakness, He can be made strong!

because of these surpassingly great revelations. Therefore, in order to keep me from becoming conceited, I was given a thorn in my flesh, a messenger of Satan, to torment me. Three times I pleaded with the Lord to take it away from me. But he said to me, "My grace is sufficient for you, for my power is made perfect in weakness." Therefore I will boast all the more gladly about my weaknesses, so that Christ's power may rest on me. That is why, for Christ's sake, I delight in weaknesses, in insults, in hardships, in persecutions, in difficulties. For when I am weak,

Once Broken

then I am strong.

2 Corinthians 12:7-10

9

The No Quit Zone

You see through all of this, I couldn't allow pride to be the dictating factor of whether I ran from my demons or whether I allowed God to be God. I going to be who I said I was or was I going to crumple at the sight of trouble?

A year ago to the date on December 18, 2014, God gave me a word. I kept hearing this phrase: *"Eminent domain."* So, I looked it up. Eminent Domain means the power to take private property for public use by a state, municipality, or private person or corporation authorized to exercise functions of public character, following the payment of just compensation to the owner of the property.

As I continued to read, I also saw another phrase: *"Inverse condemnation"* which is a term used in the law to describe a situation in which the government takes private property, but fails to pay the compensation required by the 5th Amendment of the Constitution. In some states, the term also includes the damaging of property as well as taking it.

So God says we go through life living life as we see fit. We open doors that should have never been opened because we have free will to choose; but it's not what God had planned for our lives. What I believe God is saying right now in this season to His people. "It's ok" regardless of the choices you have made in the past, you have the authority to choose and decide who the Head of your life is. Is it you, is it the enemy, or is it Christ? He is saying,

" I Am the Alpha and the Omega, the beginning and the end, the ruler of all things. You tried it your way and it didn't work, so now let's use (inverse condemnation!) You need to sue the enemy for all of the lack and death that has taken place in your life and now it's time to allow (God) to take over and have "eminent domain" over the course of your life." The definition states the power to take over property with "just payment" for that property.

That day I made a choice a choice

to resign as CEO of my own life and give You (God) "Eminent domain." He didn't just pay for me. He paid the ultimate price! He sacrificed his son for me.

He created the safety that runs through my veins because of the blood that was shed for me. You see every day there is pressure: pressure from the world, pressure from your peers, pressure from the enemy, even pressure from ourselves, but every single day, we are also given a choice, a choice to choose "free will."

This day I call the heavens and the earth

as witnesses against you that I have set before you life and death, blessings and curses. Now choose life, so that you and your children may live.

Deuteronomy 30:19

"Free will" is to allow Jesus blood to flow through our veins. If you put a tunicate on your arm, you can stop or constrict the flow of blood, or in this case stop the flow of the true and living Word of God. On the flip side, you can stop choking the Spirit of God and take that tunicate off and allow it to lead you down the path of righteousness.

Once Broken

God used murderers, whores and thieves in the Bible. What makes you think He can't use you or me! He brought Lazarus back from the dead. It is because he saw in me what I didn't see in myself that I choose to take off my grave cloths. I will serve the true and living God, through the blood, sweat, tears, lost and gains. I serve Him!

10

Closing Remarks

This walk that we walk is not called a "faith walk" for no reason.

Now faith is the substance of things hoped for, the evidence of things not seen.

Hebrews 11:1

We all literally have to walk out our faith daily even when we fall short. It is not about the number of times we fall but more so about the number of times, we get back up again; as long as we rise with a clean heart, we can begin anew again. We are the ones who turn and run because of our pride or what we deem as shortcomings. However, the God we serve sees beyond all our faults and all of our shortcomings. All he wants is a, " Yes."

You see we have all been broken at some point in life or another, but I choose to share my continual story with you because I too was once broken, but I choose to surrender to Christ. I look back at that little girl that was "once broken" by molestation, that teenager that was, "Once broken" through having a drug addicted mother, or the grown woman that was "once broken" through homosexuality, but decided to choose Christ. No matter what it looked like, no matter how dark my days got, I still choose Christ and I will continue to choose Christ.

So I challenge whoever reads this book to say, "Yes" to Christ. You are right on time and watch God move mountains on your behalf!

www.ingramcontent.com/pod-product-compliance
Lightning Source LLC
Jackson TN
JSHW021040250525
84895JS00002B/54